Early Advanced Piano

Contemporary Christian and Hymns for Weddings

9 Favorite Selections for Ceremonies

Arranged by Jan Sanborn

Contemporary Christian Songs and Hymns for Weddings contains 9 favorite songs arranged for solo piano. These arrangements are lyrical in style and can be used in wedding ceremonies or at receptions. Each arrangement has been carefully edited and fingered for performance ease. This book is a valuable resource for wedding pianists since the most popular contemporary Christian songs and hymns are included in one volume. Both the wedding party and guests will enjoy the beautiful melodies and lush harmonies of these timeless favorites.

Contents

Be Thou My Vision	9
Household of Faith	20
How Beautiful	2
I Will Be Here	12
In This Very Room	24
Love Will Be Our Home	36
O Perfect Love	32
Take My Life (Holiness)	28
When Love Is Found	16

Copyright © MMIX by Alfred Publishing Co., Inc.
All rights reserved. Printed in USA.
ISBN-10: 0-7390-5188-1
ISBN-13: 978-0-7390-5188-7

How Beautiful

Words and Music by Twila Paris
Arr. Jan Sanborn

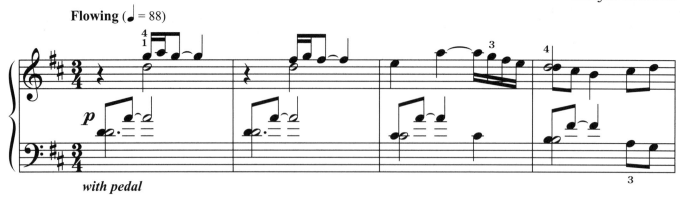

© 1990 ARIOSE MUSIC and MOUNTAIN MAGIC MUSIC
Administered by EMI CMG PUBLISHING
All Rights Reserved   Used by Permission

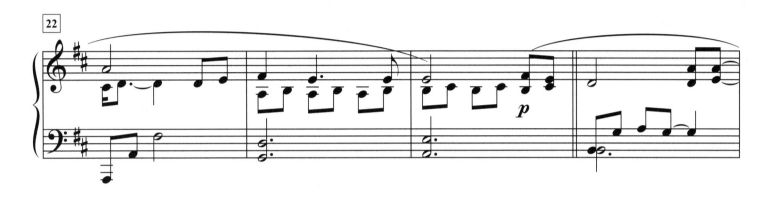

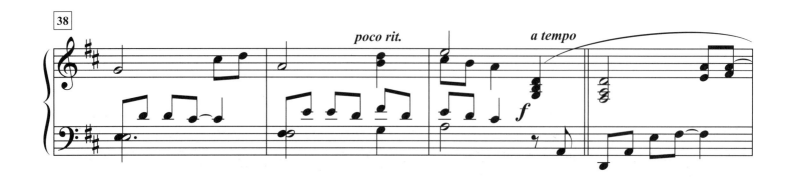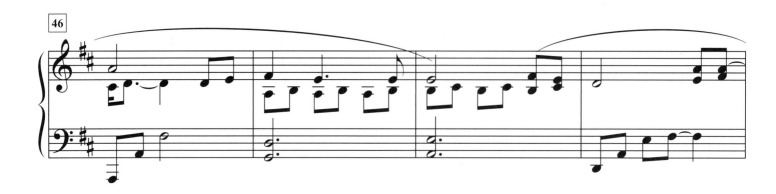

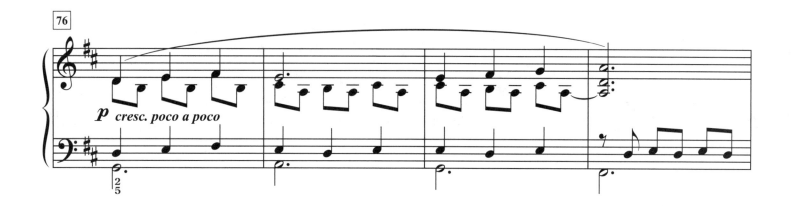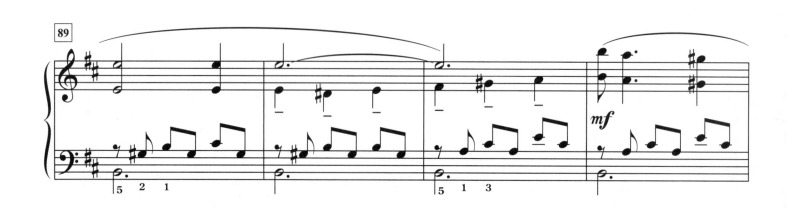

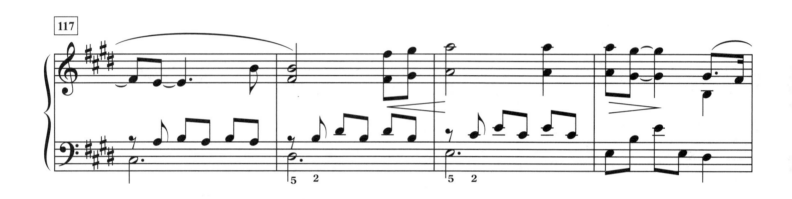

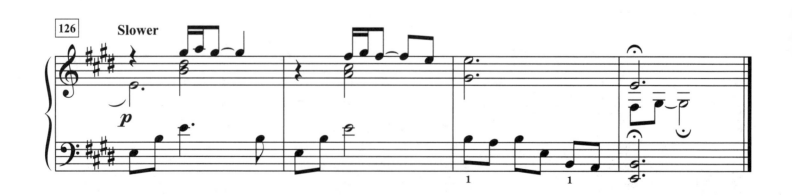

Be Thou My Vision

Traditional Irish Hymn
Arr. Jan Sanborn

I Will Be Here

Words and Music by
Steven Curtis Chapman
Arr. Jan Sanborn

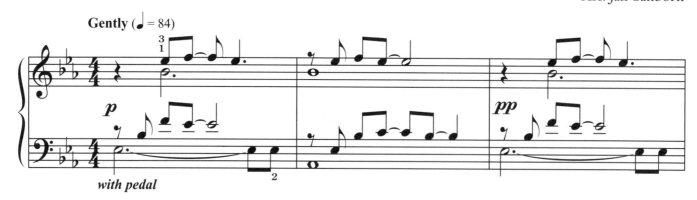
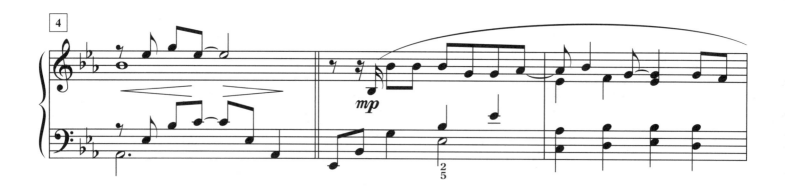

© 1990 SPARROW SONGS/CAREERS—BMG MUSIC PUBLISHING INC./GREG NELSON MUSIC
All Rights on Behalf of SPARROW SONG and GREG NELSON MUSIC administered by EMI CMG PUBLISHING
All Rights Reserved   Used by Permission

When Love Is Found

Traditional English Melody
Arr. Jan Sanborn

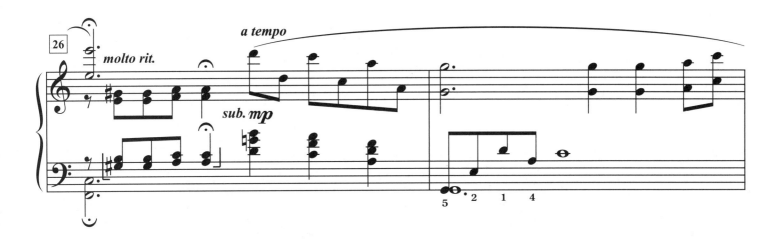
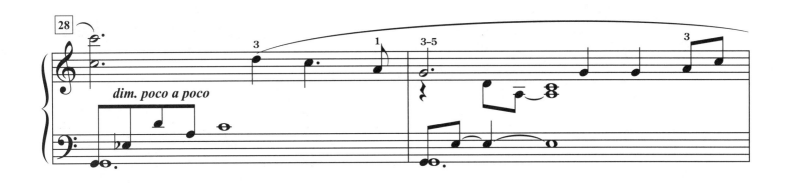

Household of Faith

Words by Brent Lamb
Music by John Rasasco
Arr. Jan Sanborn

© 1983 STRAIGHTWAY MUSIC
Administered by EMI CMG PUBLISHING
All Rights Reserved   Used by Permission

In This Very Room

Words and Music by
Ron and Carol Harris
Arr. Jan Sanborn

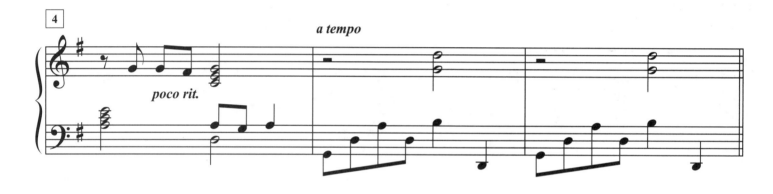

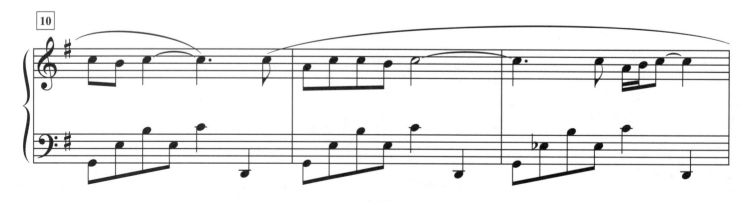

© 1979 RON HARRIS MUSIC
All Rights Reserved   Used by Permission

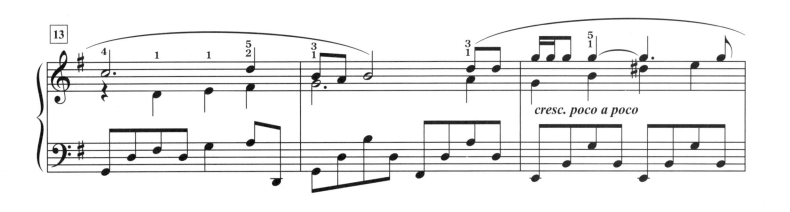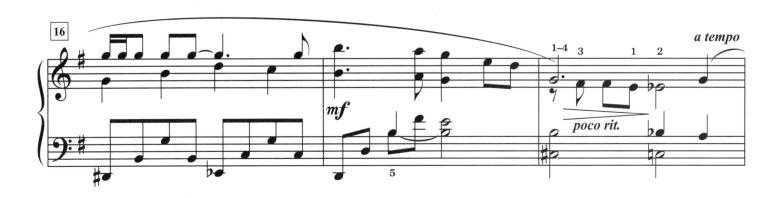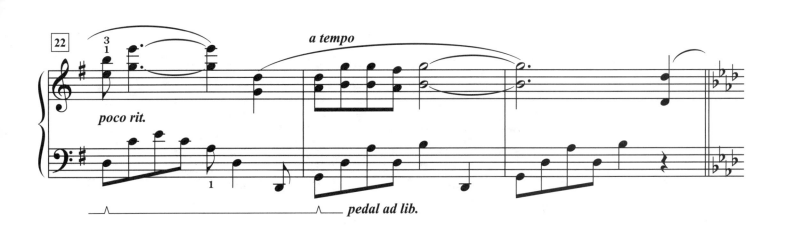

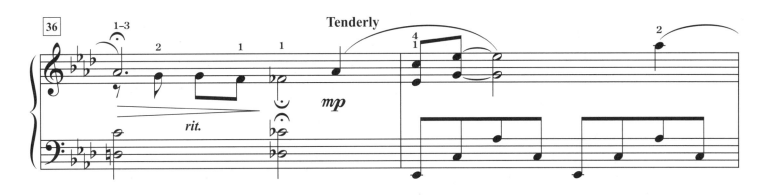
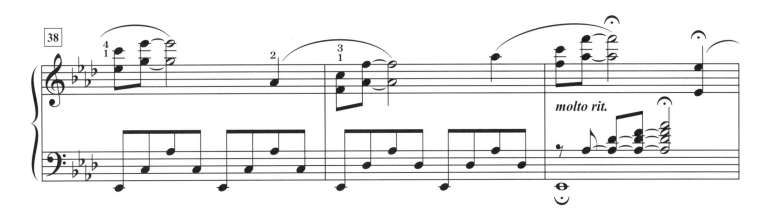
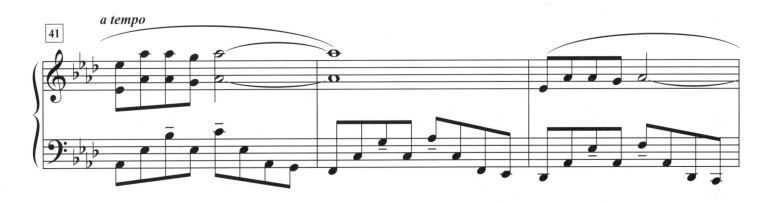

Take My Life (Holiness)

Words and Music by
Scott Underwood
Arr. Jan Sanborn

© 1994 MERCY/VINEYARD PUBLISHING
All Rights in North America Administered by MUSIC SERVICES
All Rights Reserved   Used by Permission

O Perfect Love

Words and Music by Joseph Barnby
and Dorothy Gurney
Arr. Jan Sanborn

Love Will Be Our Home

Words and Music by
Steven Curtis Chapman
Arr. Jan Sanborn

© 1994 CAREERS—BMG MUSIC PUBLISHING INC./GREG NELSON/SPARROW
All Rights Reserved   Used by Permission